THE POET WALKS AWAY

Poems by Alice Carey Alsup

PEMBERLEY
PRESS
CORONA DEL MAR

PEMBERLEY PRESS
436 Begonia Avenue
Corona del Mar, CA 92625
www.pemberleypress.com

ISBN 1-978-935421-03-0

Cover photograph: "The Passing of Time" by Kristen Danae
Keilman
Cover design by Pemberley Press

Library of Congress Cataloging-in-Publication Data

Alsup, Alice Carey.
  [Poems. Selections]
  The poet walks away : poems / by Alice Carey Alsup.
    pages cm
  ISBN 978-1-935421-03-0 (pbk. : alk. paper)
  I. Title.
  PS3601.L696A6 2015
  811'.6--dc23
                                    2014050282

CONTENTS

PART III – EARLY POEMS OF CHILDHOOD (2000 – 2008)

PART I

"LOVE POEMS"

(November – December 2013)

CONCERNING LOVE ON THE OCCASION
OF AN APOCALYPSE
(Nov 18, 2013)

It is midnight in the city of time
sometimes the expression of space is sticky.
Collaborations in translation,
they're just no longer painful.
Here's a salute to not collaborating
or even coping with the catalogue of changes to the world.
The coastline of typeface,
that museum of mountains.
Your hands are like wandergesellen—
the journeymen between us,
more or less unparalleled
as a weapon.
You are an animal catalyst
my one constant now
In the more or less toxic trade-off
that resulted from all the terrifying pesticides
and nuclear asteroids.
And every bumblebee is dead.

It can't be fall again—
one year of border crossing,
ongoing, incoming on every continent
exposed and totally captivating.
and the scientists
whet their medieval appetites
for engineering technical platforms
to rebuild us,
but all I wanted was to hear your heartbeat in my ear.
It's the whole of humanity, treated as compliant genetic collateral.

HALLOWEEN AS A HONEYMOON
(Nov 18, 2013)

I haven't held a hand,
since the era of puppy love.
Men lend themselves to me in other ways.
We take vacations from our isolation
inside of each other's bodies
Interlocking orifice with crevice,
cavity and appendage.
There's never any intimacy in the act of it.

It's hard to take back your last name
or number or a hand,
once those things have been offered.
You can always find someone
who won't ask for them.

I don't remember how to let love in tenderly;
it's always come knocking as a stranger, in costume,
Begging of me something sweet.
Love comes to me like a trick-or-treat.

I dress my windows in curtains on October 31st.
I darken my doorstep.

Some people say it's the best night of the year,
but Halloween is too fucking familiar for me.
I hide instead.
I don't like to invite comparisons
between my disguises everyday
and those people wearing
their indecencies for one night only.
"Sexy Hulk" meets "Scarlet Harlot Witch,"
No one needs to go home lonely.

Halloween is our honeymoon with anonymity.
A holiday romance, with candy corn.
The groom is in disguise.
The bride is a mystery.

It seems the only hands held are children's.
As they cross streets, roaming door-to-door.
They're seeking treats to rot their teeth.
Cavities that will one day be filled.

GEMINI
(Dec 2, 2013)

My sister doesn't like me,
Never has and she's the first to admit it.
So when a friend pit us against each other,
And she wouldn't take my side
I didn't think anything of it,
Until she said she couldn't even see where I was coming from.

But I thought we'd come from the same soil,
It had ripened in the heat of mid-Summers,
and we'd been sung to in our mother's arms by June bugs.

Lately it seems that she's been salting the earth behind my back.
Because it's been 17 months since we've spoken.
I've been counting them out in my mind,
Like trying to name stars in a dark summer sky.
She has eyes that are impossible to stare at for long.
A scowl to wither anyone who tries.
Long blonde hair, the body I will never have.
And sometimes I dream that there are two of her
Both equally unforgiving and venomous.
My mother says that I must be dreaming of her
As the two twins of Gemini,
Princes Castor and Pollux of ancient Sparta.

Born to sweet Lena, but they had different fathers.
Something called heteropaternal superfecundation,
And I swear to you it happens in 2.4% of paternity suits.

Pollux was Zeus' because that god had seduced their mother as a swan.
After his brother died in battle
Pollux went to his father broken-hearted and said
"Papa, let me share my immortality with him."

Zeus complied. He halved that everlasting life in twain
And made them the two brightest stars in a heavenly constellation
We call Gemini.

According to the horoscope, she is an air sign,
 Meaning long-winded, full of hot (yes) air.
In Astrology I am Cancer – the crab boiling as she breathes on me.
Dancing frantic in a sauce pan as she ratchets up the heat

First born into the world, she's so ready to believe it's hers,
That I don't deserve to be in it.
My father's pride is in her.
I am a mistake, shackling him to my mother,
Whose womb was only leased to me by the prior occupant.

She left the air-conditioning blasting on her way out.
But took away every blanket.
I spent my first nine months freezing,
So I will never call her heat entirely unwelcome.

But there are some things I want to tell her.
That she's a bitch more often than she isn't.
I don't miss the disparagement.
That she should go ahead and hate me,
as long and as hard as she wants to.
That I swear I won't forgive her for it.

Because who am I to take away her indignation with my
forgiveness?
With my forgiveness?
So I keep harboring her in my heart like a grudge,
And counting out every fault in our stars.

AN OVERTURE OVER INDIAN FOOD
(Dec 2, 2013)

The extent to which I want to take your hand in mine is terrifying.
We are at dinner, I know it's only a second date,
But tonight this urge won't abate, and I'm thinking about it
As we debate how best to split our appetizer,
How, if you'd allow it, I may have to hold your hand into
nothingness.

We're talking naan-stop, I could never let you go
Cause you are the spice of life
And I swear I'm never like this with anyone.

The nothingness of no one else,
And frighteningly, it's seeming like you could mean that to me
If you wanted to and no one else has ever had that option.
It's a power over me that I don't understand.

Only I've ever known what my body hungers for,
I've never seen it listed on any menu.
But I look at you and you look like the type
to end my famine.

Cause you're trouble, capital T, yet I can see your inner decency
Like everything else about you is made of tissue.

Behind your paper skin I see the fingertips of your soul.
They are itching to tangle up in my hair,
Tilting upwards the back of my head as you cradle it.
And I want us to bump our beautiful foreheads instead of uglies.
Even though I bruise way too easy, and I may grow a sore spot.
Know I spent days hoping that I would,
That this could be the type of impact you would make on me.
Love is supposed to be a bumpy tumult.

We're eating Indian tonight,
I watch you wipe the lentil daal off your chin,
Wondering if saffron stains skin, how does that taste?
How would it pair with the sweet milk kheer on my lips?
My mouth tastes of cardamom, and pistachios,
When I'm with you a fuse in my head blows.
Something about you being near
makes my stomach do backflips.
I doubt that has anything to do with the saag paneer.
Unclenching tendons in a hand that too long formed fists,
And considering closing away inches between your arm and my
wrist.
When I am near you, everything cinches,
But nothing feels wrong.

I only mean the best by it when I tell you, you are terrifying.
And when your hand moves for mine first,
I really think this is what it is to be flying.

Everything I never understood about Love,
I am learning over the course of an Indian dinner.

SALT AND PEPPER PREFACE TO A LOVE POEM
(Dec 4, 2013)

I think of my idea of love as a weathered wooden table,
Sturdy and smooth, but run your palms against the grain
And you may then spend hours removing the many splinters.
But you find words to act as tablecloths,
Silverware metaphors, and napkin allusions to pop fiction.
Salt and Pepper shakers sounding out caution, add them to taste.

Everyone adult has things they feel they could've known before
We've faced them ourselves in battle.
There aren't lesson plans or poems enough
to teach us all about how we are often devastating ourselves.
You grew up with these ideas written into songs that frightened you,
Scared you so much you put them in your playlists
Just to keep having opportunities to skip over them again.
They remind you of the faces of people who've given up
and gotten angry over time.
Those people who never tire of chasing you with taunts.
Some fears are less frightening and we're better off
Once they've been explicated.
Most of what I am speaking about is pain.
Let me revisit my own wounds now, as a lesson.
If it isn't, I have misunderstood the meaning of
Words, of what they are supposed to do for us.

It might be a thing you only understand
Once it has wounded you.
It has wounded everyone, or one day, it will.
Don't try to step out of its way,
it has no bounds and it's after our blood.

Forgive yourself for every failure in advance.
The fault was written first into our favorite fictions.

They wanted to take your faulty hopes away from you,
wished for you to aim above the real targets, to miss the marks.
Let me tell you what I know about overcorrecting,
It only steers you somewhere safer.
I don't think everyone has roadmaps to point out
the path of total destruction, but it's up ahead at the fork.
Not everyone's autopilot will always turn in that direction,
I want to believe most of us won't.

Sometimes your heart will hurt you, just because it wants
to experience that sensation of devastation.
Pain is a feeling, it's just like any other.
Triggers adrenaline like a dope needle, morphine drip.
Rushes through your bloodstreams like a river
into your seas of disappointment.
Do not get lost floating on your back,
Carried by its current.

You aren't alone if you like the pain a little,
none of us is in a world like this one. That's just impossible.
Considering your tears as bodies of water,
Ones which gravity dictates, controlling the downward directed flow,
bound by tides determined by the moon.

Don't let your mind see its grief or even the elation
as a feeling that is an exception,
Let that be a rule for love, that there's nothing exceptional about it.
And then teach that to the children who follow you.
Go back to concentrating on the appreciation
Of all of what we share.

Your heart is a cunning creature,
No less so in how it hunts, even when you are at your happiest.
It feeds each and every piece of heartbreak into the love that
follows it,

Bit by bit, while you are sleeping.
Your expectations that everything is ultimately awful
will grow on that diet until they are as high as your hopes.
Tell yourself that muscles—even the heart—are strong and
insulated.
Remember that they do not break.
The broken things are feelings; those die and are born again every day.
Let them be ephemeral, they will rise off of you and disperse.
Your heart can be as light as feathers on an arrow made of balsa wood.
I know the path that goes against love.
I often run along it, perpendicular to the direction I ought to.
And I won't recommend it, to anyone, but this is its review.
Because I need to tell you things no one ever told me.
There are certain things that you will come of age to love,
not yet having realized.
We don't learn everything right off of the bat,
or from a book in any library.
Love doesn't sound out as sharply on pages, and televisions turn the
messages into mush before they have lit up in your eyes.
I only hope to do you justice with what words come to mind.
I'm laying what I'm saying to you down on you—you as a kindness.

You learn some things from poetry.
I think we ought to mention certain types of damages, but we don't.
There are no insurance plans that cover them.
I don't know why they don't exist.
We are old enough to recognize a wrongdoing,
We must not always see it when
we are doing them to ourselves.
But we can try to.

POEM I REGRET ONLY WRITING ONCE
(Dec 5, 2013)

You have turned me into the clouds of cream in our coffee mugs.
I imagine we are drinking earl grey, Americana,
but maybe it's chicory and dirt.
I dreamed up the first seven ways I need to have you up and down.
I see sideways, standing, rough hands, few kisses.

I have twisted my dough into a crumpled piece of paper,
in more ways than one, I suspect.
I'm betting neither of us knew what to do about this.
But we had gone too deeply inside of each other's spirit caves to go
back.
I know I couldn't ever have been so ready to let someone inside.
You've already been in my cavern, you winter there to hibernate.
I refuse not to count these seasons just because we'd been asleep,
dreaming,
composing ourselves in preparation for fate's introduction.
Fate's schedule was unsatisfying, I missed you all Spring and Summer.
Passed Fall as if I were Persephone.

A sex-ed speaker once used two velcro gloves to explain what love is.
And in doing so she intervened in my life early enough,
that I might be prepared for my sensation of you.
I imagine we've skipped three bases already,
too anxious in anticipation of visiting our new hometown of Mecca.

It's not until this encounter I've ever stared so deeply into a pair of
eyes,
tested the taste of your skin with my rough tongue, a kitten's.
There will be no chastity in our exchange,
but don't consider this as anything instead of a gift-exchange.
Every part of this poem, and so many more things,
dawn on me during our hug goodnight.

We are upside down now,
incapable of taking in ourselves,
just because we are too busy occupying each other.

My cave was always such a secret space.
Spelunkers have been few and interspersed far between each other.
I've been celibate for more time than sexually active
I've had my skeleton closet to hide in until
you pushed open its door and my lungs flushed with fresh air.

DEPART FROM LEAF
(Dec 7, 2013)

twigtech:
i'm mournful
fairy lightning
singing, far
& all quaking
in delicate
slimes.
my dream
of always
beginning has
the torque
of a hand,
emptying.
The physics of our aching hearts.

Note: Critical Theory Buzzwords as Coping Mechanisms
twigtech:
post-post-continental anti-rationalist appropriation aesthetics,
ontologized sublimity of affect-networks, augmented spiritual-
ity, the withdrawal of the identified-object into an abundance of
the sensory (there are always more affects than objects/objects are
multiply-anchored w/ affects) . . .
micro-commentary on my disaffected reality.

I AM NOT IN LOVE WITH YOU
(Dec 13, 2013)

1. i am not
    in love
    with
    you.

          2. i am in
    love with
    the idea
    of you.

                    3. and frankly,
    that is the
    worst way
    to love
    someone.

I've done it so many times, too

HUNGER GAME OF HEARTS
(Dec 13, 2013)

There is no Katniss Everdeen in love,
Though love is something we've always personified
as a young boy practicing archery on us.
I don't give a shit that his mom
was the supposed goddess of Love,
who would ever give that type of arrow to a child?

I don't know what you've heard about the hunger games
we play with our hearts in the loves in our real lives.
But no one is ever accidentally prepared by their tribulations,
to be the greatest victor ever to stop the hearts
of everyone else in the area.
We will all be tributes, for the rest of all our lives.
In terms of Reapings, the only Reaper is grim.
And I've heard it said that,
"To live in the hearts we leave behind, is not to die."
I know some of us believe that we love after death,
so, the games of starvation and
of feeding on love
may never end.

I'm sorry if when your cannon rang, when your time was up,
you hadn't found a love so important it kept going.
Lots of us never do,
but that's not to say it's excusable.

There is no Katniss Everdeen in the game
of hungry, hungry hearts,
she never seemed to know her own anyway.
There is no way to take down five birds at one time,
no bow is strung ready to do that.

So, I'm Team Haymitch.
He was the only one with real advice
on the consequences of having people break your heart,
or having people that you love,
people that evil will damage
just to be sure that you will be broken.

We don't hit every mark with every arrow,
how could a baby boy with chubby fingers?
We all know somebody Cupid has fucked over at some point.
Don't read too much into love.
Don't think it will be found in any
young adult fiction.

STICKY NOTE LOVE POEM
(Dec 15, 2013)

A thousand post-it notes
are stuck onto my heart
like it's a cork board.
Leave a message,
I will read later,
and then keep,
so I can always remember
what you meant to me then.
What we meant to each other,
at one time.
Sticky notes were the invention
of two men at 3M— their names were
Art Fry and Spencer Silver.
Those men will never know
the impact they had
on my favorite organ.
How it's canary yellow now.
I swear, I don't hold it against you
that you felt the need to paste my heart
with impermanent adhesive
3 inch square paper love poems.
Neither of us thought we would
keep going this way,
until my heart was covered up with them.
It's not your fault that it's covered up still,
I could peel them off.
It wouldn't sting.
They are designed to never do that.
But I kind of like
how it's like armor.
So I don't think I will.

SUBSTANCE USE DISORDER
(Dec 17, 2013)

I'm dealing with a disease.
It's actually an epidemic,
something called a Substance Use Disorder.
Here's how to identify the infected:
We stand in clusters, furiously smoking cigarettes,
outside the basements of your houses of worship
and your friendly neighborhood YMCAs
at times of day too inconvenient to be in the act of worship,
Or to be taking a swim or attending a pilates class.
You'll find my kind on the streets,
the most desperate of us call them our homes.
Monstrosities, we know that's how some of you see us.
You should know that a lot of us spend hours
in the recesses of your community spaces,
Trying to fight our freakishness.

Tonight I am a voice of the anonymous.
Hi, my name is Alice. I am an addict.
An addict.
That's the popular vernacular, isn't it?
It's what everyone calls these endemic motherfuckers.
Only, it's not the actual word for us.
Not the definition in the DSM or any medical textbook.
You won't find any of the Drug & Alcohol policy advocates
calling what we fight everyday "addiction"
This is a terminology used to terrorize.

So we use substances disorderly,
but who doesn't, when the mood strikes?
Think of addicts as lightening rods
in a thunderstorm of substances.
One in Ten in America fits this typecast,

abuses alcohol or illicit drugs.
So, we are here, and I know that's scary,
but, I swear to you
that you'll find us everywhere.

I'm about to break our code of secrecy.
Because, I believe that when everyone of us
has a family member, or a close friend,
dealing with these demons,
you cannot imagine us away as monsters.

I've been keeping clean for months.
I've taken twelve steps away from who I was.
Because I popped and inhaled
whatever I bought, into my body.
Because, I was sold when somebody told me
that certain substances are made of miracles.
That self-medicating was a holistic alternative
to being shrunk by a psychiatrist instead.
Do not tell me I'm a villain, I am not a fiend.
My life used to be the horror story
of what my frightening whims turned me into.

Too many of ten percent of the everyday masses are "monsters,"
hiding under our bed of substances.
How do you call us disquieting?
Why tell us to silence ourselves?
No one says that to chocoholics or sex addicts,
but they are likewise seeking out inappropriate ways
to cover up what they are feeling.

I've never felt the need to get high.
I was never headed in that direction.
I used to self-destruct.
It was a way I split my thoughts into a thousand subjects,

I'd find a fix so I couldn't fixate on any one idea,
like, what's with my self-hatred?
Why don't I believe that I'm beautiful?
I cannot even see myself through your eyes anymore.
They are too occluded by the cataracts in your critiques,
I would never call your opinion an explanation.
We've spent well over a century as freaks,
shunted into your sanitariums,
cloaked in our claim to anonymity.

I know a lot of anonymous folks
better than my family knows me.
Sometimes my father still looks at me funny
when I say I used to use to stop shaking around strangers.
I don't know their last names, but,
there isn't anyone in my NA meetings
who doesn't understand that thought when I share it.

Look closer, because you are not our betters.
You may never acquit me,
may never equate yourself with an addict.
Just, let me accept myself
as more than some sick monster,
introducing herself to you tonight.
I'm not a lightening rod, under the weather
with a slight case of Substance Use Disorder.

Take me in, take this in:
all any of us ask for
is your acceptance.

FLOODGATE
(Dec 19, 2013)

Too many people tell me
they've never heard anyone talk
the way I do.
It makes them look at me like I'm different.
I'm pretty sure my heart works
the same way as theirs.
It's just that lately a floodgate broke inside of me.
So I've started saying whatever I goddamn think to.
I've started bleeding out symbolism,
Choking up imagery like phlegm.
A lover tells me subtlety isn't my thing,
I retort that mystery must be allergic to me.
He laughs, and I realize it'll be
everyone's favorite line in his next poem.
And I wouldn't mind,
except it seems that everybody
is always writing me off
into a love poem, a song.
Calling me a muse.
Like, my art will never be enough
on its own.

STOMACH ACHE
(Dec 20, 2013)

I watch a woman taking a selfie
suck in her abdomen.
It makes me slouch my spine
into an even curlier question mark.
Who pours over pictures of
such a beautiful woman
to judge the jut of their gut?
Why would that say anything
about the person posing
in the photo?
I'm concerned for those people
asking these questions.

I push my pelvis forward,
and dare to look full.
I'm not implying that
this road was easy.
I'd liken it to your first 5K.

Cause I spent high school skinny.
Skimpy off of 50 mg
Adderall XR breakfast,
lunch of self-loathing,
afternoon snack of 15 mg
Adderall immediate release.
It was a physician-endorsed
amphetamine diet.
Socially accepted
body dysmorphia.
It simplified my
irrational hunger strike,
power trip disorder.

I loved to deny myself.
Pinched away impossible centimeters.
I think I "body-checked" more often
than the All-state Varsity
Lacrosse team.

I still beat drum lines
on my collarbones
when I'm nervous.
But I don't run my fingers
along my ribcage
like it's a zydeco.
I won't let myself see
bodies as trophies.
Part of me still feels
that I lost that contest
the day I hit 110.
I'm not trying to take
that number down again.
I thought I found that empowering,
but the ideas are empty.

I've learned a lot,
gained the weight of wisdom.
I won't mind if you
feel the need to take
a moment to applaud
my learning curve.

CHILDREN OF GOD
(Dec 21, 2013)

This is a poem I never planned to pen,
until, over a drink, he tells me about the girl
I noticed him watching from our pew.
She goes to his 11 am ecclesiastic service,
and I swear she does it, in part,
just to ignore him.
His eyes light up as he explains how,
this past Sunday,
she offered him her handshake
and a "may Peace be with you."
I take steady sips of my wine and start to wonder
if what happened is that she saw him through me.
I know I stuck out of that Sunday service
like a sore thumb sticks out of its palm.
Shakespeare called palm-to-palm
holy palmer's kiss.
But, I've never held his hand.
He's never offered it.

That was the Sunday I gave God one last shot.
This man I silently adored
stepped up to take me to his church.
I chose him as my shepherd;
I've always felt like a part of his flock.
Did she wonder if she might no longer be his preoccupation,
if he fell for a doubt-filled question mark disbeliever like me?
That he would forget his favorite, his faithful period.
That peaceful piece to end his every doubt.

She has no reason to worry that he will ever
stop sneaking looks at her,
whenever he thinks she is too absorbed in a psalm
to notice the impiety in his glances.

I watched him staring at her
throughout a sermon entitled,
"On the love in our hearts for every child of God."

I always fight the urge,
of how much
I want him to hold me in his heart.
I've prayed I could be his punctuation mark,
whatever character to take away any disbelief.
But I know that no amount of my devotion
will ever make him hold me as if I am anything,
except another one of every child of God.

JESSE WILLMS, DARK LORD OF THE INTERNET
How one of the most notorious alleged hustlers in the history of
e-commerce made a fortune on the Web
Never knew this guy was out there, fueling my hate fire.

TO JESSE WILLMS
(Dec 26, 2013)

Dear Jesse—
Thank you for defrauding the global economy
of at least 500 million dollars.
For the credit card fraud,
and all those pseudo-pharmaceutical scams.

Thanks for the Shake Weight.
For those Green Tea Acai Diet Pills,
the ones I took until I passed out,
and then kept in my kitchen cupboard,
just in case.

For what you did to ecommerce,
and to consumer confidence,
Truly, from the bottom of my piggy bank,
thank you.

We all needed another reason to doubt.
What's one more cringe-worthy charge
on our credit card statements?

I want you to know
that I joined Wikipedia this morning.
That my only intent in doing so
was to illuminate you.

The Dark Lord of the Internet.

It's time we celebrate the creeps,
The crooks that have preyed on everything
anyone's ever secretly loathed
about themselves:
Our less-than-brilliant smiles,
the dimples in our derrieres.

I never did learn that one simple trick
For reducing your belly fat.
But I never gave you my 16 digit identity,
so I guess I'll never know.
I guess this makes us even.

I guess I wish there were a hell for you to rot in forever.

From the desk of your biggest fan.

AFTER THAT FIGHT
(Jan 18, 2014)

Wait eight days to call. Suggest that you two make dinner at his
place.
When you show up, look beautiful. (You are so beautiful.)
Ask to choose one of his records to play.
Pick something foreign. Something funky.
Sing along, if only to remind him how much he loves your voice.
Cook something with chili peppers in it
and add Sriracha like it is ketchup.
Volunteer to chop up the onions, in case he ends it
over the course of your kitchen prep work.
Talk about the poems you have been writing and
how happy you are that life has been getting a little bit hectic
lately.
Wait patiently for him to bring up the subject of 'us'.
Don't allow him to apologize.
Remind him that he was never really in the wrong.
Say that you have been thinking about him, but you've been
too bashful to say anything after that fight. Smile sadly when he
grimaces.
Squeeze his hand and assure him that you still feel
so comfortable around him.
Say that the basis for a beautiful friendship is definitely still there.
Hope that he agrees.
If he cries while he explains that he got lost in his last relationship,
sit next to him and cry along.
Tell him about the boy who broke you.
Remind him that we are all so much more
than the sum total of our damages.
Tell him he is beautiful. (He is so beautiful.)
That he gives you hope.
Even if your mistakes have already
overwhelmed your chances,
that his heart has touched yours.

If you need to say "I love you,"
add in all those words to temper them.
"I love to be around you," "I have so much love for you."
You'll need to leave before midnight.
Cite an early morning.
Do not stay.
Remember that you may always regret
how quickly you held him all too close.
Let yourself hold him close tonight.
As if this will be your last moment in his arms.
Do not kiss him.
And when you kiss him, count to three.
It's okay to press your thumb onto his earlobe
the way you always have,
but do not linger.
Tell yourself that this is temporary,
a hiccup in the life that you will live together.
And if you cry over this goodbye, let him see those tears.
He has always told you that you are beautiful,
so beautiful even as you cry.
Thank him for the evening.
Say it in a way that says,
"thank you for every evening,
every morning."
Say goodbye.

PART II

SLAM POEMS

(January – May, 2014)

ON THE CONS OF LOSING WEIGHT
(Jan 1, 2014)

Because haven't we all heard enough lists
of the pros by now?
Why you need to lose weight.
How you need to lose weight.
What to put on your plate.
How to Look "Grrrrrreat!"
How to motivate yourself into a gym,
or a mat, or a track, or onto a scale,
or a table on which they will cut away at everything
that cushions you.

But concerning the cons, I've thought up a few:

You may find that you start holding onto yourself,
as if afraid that you will fade away.

Exes may start telling you that you look skinny
—not in a good way.

The bruises bruise uglier.
The scars look less like stretch marks.
Stretch marks more like scars.

Worrying that you are shrinking.
Worrying that you like that you are shrinking.

Measuring out your meals in half cups and calorie counts.
Feeling the absence of that missing flesh.
Feeling less and less invisible,
as boys start touching bones.
The places where the fat won't melt off of you,
Wondering where it has?

36

Where it will?

Facing down your reflection when the caverns come out
underneath your eyes, along your clavicles
and in your cheekbones.

The clothes that, having too long haunted
the back of your closet,
start coming out again like
the ghosts of fashion faux-pas past.

Public displays of appetite: meaning eating to
prove that you aren't starving.
Starving.

But if you decide to lose weight, do it right.
Don't fast. Build your body up with mass
instead of dropping dress sizes.
Do cardio so that you can walk away farther and faster away
from the people looking at you like you are an object.
Like you are wrong to be shaping yourself into something strong.

Outrun the scorn sounding in the voices that tell you you've
succumbed to fashion.
Fashion your body into a statement of strength.
Concentrate on the powerhouse of your core beliefs.

Do not listen to those people whose eyes are
an auctioneer's appraisals.
Not even those you see in your mirror.
Don't listen to anyone who will look to you
to simultaneously covet and shame.
Ad campaigns have gotten too good at
guilting us into the idea that we fit
into our own skins funny.

But own your own skin with discipline and worship and
irreverence.

Sculpt self-esteem.
Keep your epic ass and hope your tits don't disappear.

On losing weight: write a list of all the pros
for making up for in pride,
whatever you lose in inches and ounces.
Don't overdo it, don't do it for anyone but you.

Bold Face Conference, May 2014

ARACHNOPHOBIA
(Jan 18, 2014)

With the lights shut off,
windows rolled up,
wrapped in navy blue sheets,
With the hum of cicadas and the
skipping beats of a spent record
spinning out a cacophony,
he asks me what I am afraid of.

I don't tell him the truth.
Which is that I've never been afraid of
anything… apart from him.
That until the thought of the morning after
this whispered midnight chatter,
nothing has ever struck me
as particularly terrifying.

So I am lying as I tell him
that I have an arachnophobia;
that eight-legs and scorpions
and spiders scare me.
You see,
it's closer to the truth
for me to say that I
identify with them.

With thick skin, sharp pincers,
eyes that never miss much.

And they say that spiders mate for life.
I know they don't live long
but that still sounds frightening enough.

Add to that that lying next to him,
I understand the impulse.
And it's terrifying,
so I just keep lying.

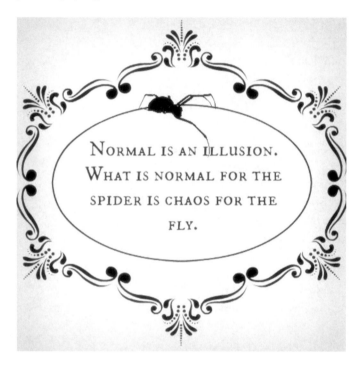

NORMAL IS AN ILLUSION.
WHAT IS NORMAL FOR THE
SPIDER IS CHAOS FOR THE
FLY.

I tell people I am an arachnid.

Bold Face Conference, May 2014

THE BRIDE OF BACCHUS
(Jan 19, 2014)

I mix honey into our wine
and we call it heaven.
Dionysus and I drink each other in
and we are never sated.
He tells me I make him feel fizzy,
he makes me dizzy,
and love isn't supposed to be sober.

The only problem is that alcohol
doesn't offer any apologies
and 'intoxicating' is a prettier way
of saying 'poisoned.'

So when our stomachs turn,
the toxins burn in our skin,
Dionysus tells me that he needs
something stronger.
So I go out,
looking for an antidote.

And at the end of it all,
after our deluge, dissolution,
he stirs battery acid
into coca cola and calls it
a fond farewell.

I drink down every drop.

Bold Face Conference, May 2014

PAGEFRIGHT
(Jan 22, 2014)

I think I'm becoming afraid of tumblr. I can't understand the relationship I want to have with having an internet identity, with laying out my bones and letting other people fill in the blanks. I've always been the type who tweaks and tweaks, nothing is ever perfected and I hate deciding whether to go back and alter those works or preserve the proof of process.

The idea that people can see so much of my naked newness in pixilated flaw form made my stomach turn last night. Vulnerability, not sure how to do it well if I spell it out on the internet but can't summon that up in real time.

SONDER
(Nov 24, 2014)

dictionaryofobscuresorrows:
n. the realization that each random passerby is living a life as vivid and complex as your own—populated with their own ambitions, friends, routines, worries and inherited craziness—an epic story that continues invisibly around you like an anthill sprawling deep underground, with elaborate…

LOVE AFFAIR WITH A NIGHTMARE
(Jan 31, 2014)

I'm looking for
a dude with
a dick like
burning sage.
You see, I need
to smoke him out
of me
somehow.
I have no idea of
how to fight
this phantom.
But I can't keep on
haunting all those
abandoned places,
in search of someone
who was never
mine.
Paranormals like to
tell you they aren't
into "parameters."
So I'm searching for a man
who can double as
a psychic.
His memory lingers,
still, on my skin;
like Dr. Braun's soap
smell and the aftertaste
of an excellent
cup of coffee.
I can't let go

of the memory
of getting weird
with all of
our clothes still on.
The way he would
look at me
like a monster
at the end of
a chase.
I'm having nightmares
of drag race
disasters.
The worst part is always
the long-haired harpy
in his passenger seat.
Sell me that
snake oil sex,
if it promises to
erase this angry
shade.
I'll trade
moonstones,
wolfsbane.
So, I'm gonna
go ahead and go out
looking for an exorcist
to fuck him out of me.
Find any way I can
to let go of
a ghost.

HOPE
(Feb 6, 2014)

We came.
We came to.
We came to believe.
That a Power greater than ourselves
could restore us to sanity.
A man named Joseph
with three missing front teeth breaks down
the 2nd step like that and realigns my universe.
Jerry chooses our meeting's topic
And it's one word: hope.
As in how does hope restore us to sanity?
Jerry had brain surgery on Wednesday
and he's back in the NA rooms on this Sunday afternoon.
He says, "if you start to feel all-powerful,
go to the ocean shore and try to stop the tides.
Cure brain cancer without chemotherapy, without surgery
after surgery, without prescribing even a single pill.
Lucky is a hipster kid just getting clean,
new to our rooms, and he inspires me when he says
he hopes to someday inspire an addict with his story of recovery.

When it's time for my share, I tell them about
how I was raised without any high hopes, about anything.
Plenty of love, but our family's way
was to argue analytics and issues at the dinner table.
The arguments for hope are few and far between,
and not particularly persuasive.
A year ago to this day I had lost every last hope.
So I took an overdose of a prescription
and tried so hard to let everything go.
But when the OD symptoms started up,
it occurred to me that I was shuffling off

this mortal coil with some unanswered questions.
Couldn't think of anyone to call, so I dialed a hotline
and I met Monica: 18, college-bound in the fall,
no history of depression or addiction and
no opinion at all about having hope or how to let it go.
But she did let me know that my call had been traced
and the cops were on their way.
So I'm alive today and still left with some questions.
I do have one hypothesis:
that addicts are born with oversized hearts.
It takes more love and yes, hope, to fill us with anything.
I don't hear a higher power, haven't since I stopped using.
But hearing Joe, Jerry and Lucky
spilling out their full hearts, I feel restored.
And you have to have hope, to surrender to sanity.

ON THE RANGE
(Feb 6, 2014)

My sister and I spent the summers of our youths
at a cabin in the woods beside a horseshoe-shaped lake.
Two little big city girls camping out in the country,
can you imagine how magical it was?
We made finger paint trail maps and played all the usual games:
pioneer women living on the range,
how many minnows can you catch with just a hook and a grub?
Who can hold her breath underwater longest?
It's crazy how many different ways children can find to have fun.
I went up to that cabin after she pulled a Ted Kaczynski
and got Committed.
I was cleaning up any evidence of her illness.
What I found was that her brand of insane is just the same as
mine.
Washing lipstick graffiti messages off of the walls
addressed to an old boyfriend and to God,
my thought was, "these are just like the letters
I wrote from that Institution last year."
We move around the memorabilia of our separate lives
as if we are playing the same game of treasure mapping out our
mania.
Maybe there was something in that lake water
which both of us were drinking as the sunshine
peppered us with freckles.
There is madness burning up in us both like a bonfire.

WORD PORN POEM
(Apr 25, 2014)

I have been following a thread on Facebook,
word porn.
I thread the words through us.
Sometimes I think it's the story of us.
Holophrasis: (n) the expression of complex ideas in a single word
or phrase
This is all I'm looking for.

Kilig: (n) the rush or inexplicable joy one feels after seeing or
experiencing something romantic.
Do you remember how I read to you on stage? No, you've never
seen it.

Tarantism: (n) overcoming melancholy by dancing; the urge to
dance.
Would you dance with me if I asked you to?
Would you hold me at a distance?

Tacenda: (n) things better left unsaid; matters to be passed over in
silence.
Maybe we could dance like our lives deserved a soundtrack.
Track marks scars of Bright Eyes and Bon Iver, golden oldies.
And you call your band New Mercies, but that's what you've never
been.

Accismus: (n) feigning disinterest in something while actually
desiring it.
I don't miss you. I wouldn't trade you for the state of Texas.

Pluviophile: (n) a lover of the smell of rain.
I sought out rejection like storms seek out drought, like a renewal.
Petrichor: (n) the scent of earth after rain.
I sought you out like rain seeks soil.

Scripturient: (adj) having a consuming passion to write
Can I write you back to me?
I have written you so many sorries.

Selcouth: (adj) unfamiliar, rare, strange, and yet marvelous
You were the Johnny Walker to my Jasmine Tea.
We tasted like a sweet mistake tastes to an alcoholic.

Abditory: (n) a place into which you can disappear; a hiding place
You were trouble, and trouble never had a face like yours.
Eyes that I disappeared into. You kept them closed.

Niedosyt: (n) a lack of sufficient satisfaction of one's need.
You were forgiveness on spent sheets.
Sometimes just an anticlimactic apology.
I'm sorry for the scratches.
Do you remember how the bite marks bloomed on me like
clamshell butterfly wings?
It's because I bled too well for your teeth.
And I know my heart was hickey-shaped before it ever met yours,
scar tissue riddled.

Alexithymia: (n) An inability to describe emotions in a verbal
manner
But your laugh came with a question mark.
My lips are held up by a bow,
Quiver full of arrows, strung tight, unused.
Tips dipped in poisons of your taste.

Anagapesis: (n) No longer feeling any affection for someone
you once loved.
I am trying. You've done it so well.

Lalochezia: (n) the emotional relief gained from the use of profane
language.

Fuck you. Fuck her, I know you've fucked every cunt you could.
Lethologica: (n) when you think of something but the word for it escapes you.
What if that poem about four letter words that sting worst spell out,
L-O-V-E,
P-A-I-N,
O-V-E-R me.

Lethologica: (n) when you think of something but the word for it escapes you.
You are a dictionary too heavy for me to throw at your head.
Words unsaid.

Induratize: (v) to make one's own heart hardened or resistant to someone's pleas or advances, or to the idea of love.
Our armored hearts made war,
and I wasn't warrior enough.

Finifugal: (adj) hating endings; of someone who tries to avoid or prolong the final moments of a story, relationship, or some other journey.
Word Porn
Elegy of Us.
Enough.

EROTIC LUSTS

When we first met,
I was frantic sex,
I was "yes, get inside of me now."
Yes. I was so wet.
You were hair unkempt.
Your snarl unconcealed.
Glasses kept on.
Cause neither of us meant
to miss a moment.

And our disasters made fast friends.
Our lusts got along so well.

I was collarbone bit
to your shoulder blade cupped.
The small of my back knew the palm of your hand
like a saddle knows its horn.

But your laugh came with a question mark
and my soft body concealed sharp angles.
Our bodies had borders,
sometimes sex is a skirmish.
Sometimes it's a slaughter.

I was hair-pulled, fight-picked,
angry sex, sorry in retrospect.
You were forgiveness on spent sheets.
Sometimes just anticlimactic apologies.

But we sparred in battlefield bed
like Trojan soldiers on fulsome shores,
scarred and already readied for war.

It was rough on request.
Pin me down,
pull you back,
I cum, you cum,
fade to black.
Very little peacetime pillow talk.

Forgive me for the scratches.
Do you remember how my bite mark bruises
bloomed like clamshell butterflies?

It was because I bleed so easy,
and I know my heart was hickey-shaped,
long before our bodies clashed so beautifully.
But your sharp mouth didn't help matters much.

Maybe I shielded my ecstatic face too well.
Didn't sand down my edges fast enough.
Maybe you mistook a martial mask
for a martial mindset.
Maybe you should have fought for me.

But we just walked away
from our war, wounded.
Borders bloodied.

Our disasters made fast friends.
Our lusts got along so well.
But our appetites were eager adversaries.
You are now arched ambivalence,
forced laughter still studded with question marks,
sharp-tooth smile.
And I am quiver-loaded lips,
I am love-avoidant anger.

People love to pretend that the aftermath
of wartime is peacetime.
But our territories are chicken wire fenced.
There's no going back to indifference.

JEZEBEL

My vagina smells like shame.
And don't.
And I will if you won't.
I used to make men who'd been below my belt,
brush their teeth before I could kiss them on the mouth.
I don't want to know the taste of blame.

And odor itself is entirely irrelevant.
Varies on the moment and the month and the moon.
But it's not that my hygiene isn't immaculate.
I am not immaculate.
Not one of us is.
Jesus, even Christ was born of a woman's blood.
Women are cursed to bear us in blood.

And it has taken ages to overcome the idea
that my body is blasphemous.
That these childbearing hips
are somehow sacrilegious.

But I might just be following orders,
obeying the idea that I come at his convenience,
but his pleasure is my purpose.

Women have been taught certain commandments.
Like, that when I feel the blood
I must stop it up immediately.
Because blood only has a scent
when it hits the air.
So like a confession.
You can clean it up,
conceal its scent.
Turn down cunnilingus with every excuse except
that I won't let you see what Eve did to me.

But my mother was the one who taught me
that masturbation helps with the cramps.
That hot tea helps me ward off the menstrual migraines.
That Midol and Tylenol are the same.

We have been marketed our bloodguilt by ad men
who seem to think that what women carry
inside ourselves are tombs.

And there are myths that predate even the magazines,
but let me assure you that my pussy doesn't have teeth.
That when it turns red, it isn't blushing.
And women can swim in the ocean without the risk
of a shark attack.

I'm wondering how long ago I learned
the scripture of
"I am stained.
I am sorry.
I am so ashamed."

Because, to me, my vagina smells like shame.
But I've been told that it tastes like caramel,
sourdough bread and the yolk of an over-easy egg.
Like something tangy that isn't acid or rancid,
Because it is the taste (and smell) of Vagina.
I've met men who've told me that,
at certain times of the month,
they are willing to be werewolves.
That I need to accept my own anatomy,
and I don't know why I needed any affirmation.
Because I know that it bleeds, and secretes.
But it also comes and goes as it pleases,
And it melts on a tongue like a wafer.
Everything about that is delicious.

It isn't disgusting for a vagina
To smell like the organ that it is.

Because what my vagina actually smells like
Is secret.
It is cavern.
Cove.
Tunnel of love.
It is treasure trove.

Endeavor to deserve it,
Or don't.
But do not shame,
Or fault.

It has sacrificed enough.

Bold Face Conference, May 2014

IF THE BODY IS A UNIVERSE
(Apr 25, 2014)

Taoists have a funny way of looking at life.
They say that the body is a universe.

If that's the case, and I am a cosmos,
My veins are tiny little milky ways
carrying my blood made of the rust of exploded stars.
My heart is a nebula, birthing out a thousand more stars each day.

If the body is a universe, that means that the scars and bruises
we carry on our skin are the craters on those outlier planets,
The ones we study from our telescopes,
as we dream of terraforming brave new worlds,
There to remind us of the terrifying impacts that we have survived.
That the universe keeps ticking away like a pulse-line.

If the body is a universe, it doesn't come with apologies or excuses,
it comes with gravity and an idea of the infinite
that our human minds may never wrap around
but we can all embody.

If infinity is inherited,
my mother is the goddess I have always known her to be,
My father, the emperor he has always called himself,
My sister will always be a constellation.
And I have a birthmark the shape of Beetlejuice,
because there are galaxies in our genes.

I've never envisioned that God has any genitalia.
But we do, so maybe sex is as sacred as we are taught in our temples.
But the body is not a sanctuary.
It is a constantly dynamic Cosmos
And there's a flux in the fleshy distance between us.

If the body is a universe I don't think it knows how to say
"I'm sorry."
And I'm not.
I am all jutting out awkward cacophony.
But I'll blame my mood-swings on the moons of Neptune.
And I'll say you are being sulky because Uranus is in retrograde.

We can start re-conceptualizing compliments:
Thank you, miss, for the meteor shower in your cackle.
Excuse me sir, but you have a little north star in your smile.
Baby, your eyes are the color of Venus.

Let's call Carl Sagan a prophet;
Stephen Hawkings, a messiah wheeling among us.
We can rename Einstein St. Albert.
And none of those words will mean anything anyway.
What are titles to totalities unto themselves?

What if when we hold ourselves we are holding onto the universe?
And it is soft and fragile and animal.
Blood, bone, body.
Why would it be anything else?

Presented at Notsuoh

POEM ABOUT PRIVILEGE
(Apr 27, 2014)

This is a poem about privilege.
I've got a lot of thoughts about it,
I've got a lot more than anyone ought to have of it.
And I wanna talk about it.
Cause I've never heard anyone stand
on a stage and say this.

I am cis-gendered. Fiscally well-off.
Able-bodied, young in an age of ageism.
I've never lived in the wrong parts of a city.
I live on the right side of social biases
with which I disagree. But that doesn't matter.
Don't let white people tell you it isn't easy
to be white people.
That reverse racism exists.

I am thin enough, cute enough,
fill this in enough
to get to be a woman.
My skin is the white and pink of a peppermint.
In a world where not everyone loves chocolate,
caramel, marzipan. I do. But I don't like cinnamon.

I'm a poor little rich girl.
Pretty young thing,
I am white devil, devil on my back
because I know exactly what this is.
It's privilege.

I was born to a fortunate son and
a Daughter of the Confederacy
who, when I told her I had dated a black dude,

had three questions for me:
Does he have AIDS?
Is he a heroin addict?
Would you have wanted him if he weren't a poet?

I was silver spooned blue blood
and peachy cream cheeks have never come
with a side of apology. I am sorry.
I often wish skin were invisible.
That we wore the veins and arteries
that stitch us together like a sweater.
But skin is really just a beginning.

I have lived in a house with a white picket fence.
I live in the Third Ward now,
in what my housemates call "The Ghetto Mansion."
And I cringe, but sometimes I still joke
that I'm the face of gentrification.
And I am. And I am sorry that I stand
on this side of class warfare.
I'm sorry if I am making any of you uncomfortable.
Why aren't we all of us a little
more uncomfortable anyway?

And I can call myself heterosexual,
And if I were to say I weren't
that would make me a bisexual.
And pejorative pornography preaching
to me is appealing,

So long as I am still a woman.
I don't have deal with dirty looks
from the Ted Cruz types
or bullshit from Michelle Bachman bitches.
Michelle Bachman, who once said that,

were public schools to teach us
that homosexuality is not an aberration,
it would lead to "sexual anarchy."
Which sounds fucking sexy to me.

Underscore me 'cause I'm too privileged to be a poet.
Because this isn't a tale of woe.
I can't write those.
I am bland.
I am fit into a crowd like a jigsaw puzzle piece.
I will never be told to sand myself down,
to scythe something of me off.
I am not living proof of people
robbed of their homeland.
A WASP doesn't have a holocaust,
a genocide, bigotry, prejudice.
You see, I'm supposed to be
the one to perpetuate it.

This is a poem about privilege.
I'm sorry if it sounded a lot
more like a "humble brag."
Who wants to win at something rigged?
Who wants to feel like it's a rat race, race war?
There's a lot more to this than an apology.
There is anger looking for a way forward.
Away from mindsets like my mother's.

My skin comes with slurs like
"Poor little rich girl."
"Pretty young thing."
White devil.
Spoiled brat.
"Bitch, please… why are you even complaining?"

TRAIL MAP

Do you understand it when I tell you that
you've got the heart of a trail map.
That your soul smells something like a hickory wood campfire?
And when you told me I look like the wilderness,
I just wanted you to know that you would never find yourself lost in me.
And if you've always been an outdoors girl,
and I've always been a forest of bramble,
I want you to find your way through me,
I want to be your Appalachia.

You can trace every course of my skin, even the ones
whose tracks have been left by hunters.
You could go on great expeditions through me.
Swim the rivers of my veins, whose currents would carry you gentle.
Track boot prints on every bank, I will cake them fossil with my sun.
You are the taste of its light to a canopy of leaves.
Come into me, into this wilderness.
Because you make me feel endless,
as if impossible to cut down.

Take your telescope into the clearing of a field in my forest,
and search out every constellation.
I could show you the secrets of an infinite sky.
I will let you in, point out the scorch marks patches of wild fires.
Let you touch scars carved by bowie knives.
Because your fingertips are not mazes, but maps.
I've never met a trail map with a heart so big,
a compass so clear that there are rose stars in your eyes.
I want to know your texture, topography.

Come into me.
Into this wilderness, in which you will be loved.
And there will be other trekkers, explorers, outdoorsmen.

And you are a book of maps, so I know there will be other forests,
jungles, deserts, shorelines.

But I will always welcome you into my forest friendly, familiar.
Because you tell me you're an outdoors girl,
and that I look like the wilderness.
So this will be a great adventure.

Bold Face Conference, May 2014

DRIVING OUTSIDE OF THE HOUSTON CITY LIMITS

Driving outside of the Houston city limits,
I am listening to songs about south Texas.
There aren't enough of them.
Singin' in twangy drawl about two-steppin'
to your best friend's Klezmer band,
the laughing sound of your ex's hand on his electric guitar.
Texas is the vastness of our skies,
a field of Indian paint brushes touching everything, including the
infinite,
the work of our winters,
the smell of the wall of honeysuckles,
the strength of knowing how to be alone with family who taught
you how not to be,
it's the sound of a lover taking in a breath underneath your ear,
the feeling of your newborn niece's hand wrapped around your
finger,
the sight of your brother's bride's sweat damp curls after that child's
birth,
the scars that split the difference between you in Bryan
and I in Houston.
Nuzzling to you is feeling the pull of constellations like a lasso.
The Lone Star State is the Rio Grande, Buffalo Bayou, Colorado,
Navasota.
It is green-brown tainted, rope swinging into dawn off the dock in
the Hill Country,
waking up to a sunrise in Big Bend,
the sound of cicada summers,
sight of June bugs in flight around all those lamp posts,
There are too many isles of cement,
too many inmates up in Huntsville
too many of whom are only carried out in a body bag,
too many hipsters and immigrants from up in NYC
who came to Austin last spring, their tattoos of our state worn like
a breastplate.

But our hearts are the shape of Texas and our blood tastes like our
Arnold Palmer sweet tea,
like the joy and pain of that moment
when your cat catches the mockingbird in its teeth,
the freckles on your horse's neck.
And we will one day figure out how to forgive Dallas
for the convenience store,
the stripmalls encroaching on Amarillo.
Texas gives us the armor of the armadillo
teaches us to be as tall as the Transco Tower
or that 67 foot statue of Sam Houston,
gives us heroes like George Strait, Towns Van Zandt, ZZ Top, and
the Dixie Chicks.
Texas is the reason I write, the reason I sing along to all of those
country classics,
believe in all the folklore,
it's your heart in the sky, whose stars have never ever been alone.

PYRE POEM
(May 2014)

If everything you love, you love at first sight, about that person,
If you position your tender –arrange it as a teepee of twigs.
Crumble up love poems you read or wrote only thinking of them,
Douse out whiskey and house them in the center of your pyre.
Build them up until the pile is roughly the size of a human chest.
Light it on fire and coax tiny flames at the four corners.
Blow breaths of heartache to stoke the flames.
Whispers and coos of confession will do you no good.
There's nothing left now that goes unsaid.
With screams, I know of no sound more comforting.
Start piecing larger branches onto the pile
And smiles and stop-less parties in their morning slumbers
Their ridiculous dairy free lifestyles
Callous finger tips and whatever it is you will mourn most
You will find it in capital fuel.

Lean these larger logs against each other in the shape of a pyramid
and put it up as flames.
Burn it to the ground because this love is not a wonder of the world
It happens like this every day: this is how it ends in the night.
Breathe in the smoke, coat your lungs and throat with fire.
There's nothing left now that goes unsaid.
The wood screams and sizzles –I know of no sound more comforting
than that one.

APOPLEXY

I worry I will never be the kind of poet she needs.
What if I never speak into being that salve
to apply to whatever broke inside her?
What if I make her aches worse?
I write so many poems in the hope she will stumble upon them.
Look up, confused,
And finally see my smoke signal trails.
The ones that read,
"I'm sorry."

Still don't really know what for,
but I'm trying to reach her anyway.
This poem doesn't have any resolution.
Doesn't deserve one...
Yet

ALICE: THE ULTIMATE MANIC PIXIE DREAMGIRL

It's so tiring having to spit out
those poisons foisted on me.
I'm tired of shrinking until
I am under the table or shooting up
until I shatter that glass ceiling.
Do you know why there are
ceiling tiles made of mirror?
 It's the only way to be sure
of never falling inside of them.

Don't go asking for me to introduce myself.
I will try to lie to you.
I seek only comfort in my mistruth,
I cannot lay my name on you,
not in a way either of us will understand.
Alices have too many antique connotations.

I like reflecting, but I fear mirrors
like fox traps.
I hate the hares like hound dogs.
I'm still suspicious of the red queen.
See, I think she still chases me
in my dreams with a shiv
fashioned from a croquet mallet.
But the thing she seeks is Alice's
untouched heart.
She just can't travel back in time,
Not far enough to reclaim
her own innocence again.
Even in dreams I skin knees and elbows,
still fall so hard down into that rabbit hole.
You wouldn't believe the frightening things
that are suspended in that rabbit's nest,
and I fall into it every time.

There must be reasons
why Alice never found a love interest
as she wandered around wonderland.
Lewis Caroll must have felt too much for her
to introduce to her a character
not fixated on keeping a schedule,
chained to his wristwatch,
maddened by mercury poisoning
or a set of twins too busy
twiddling their thumbs
to try to comprehend her.

Manic pixie dream girls are creatures
that exist only in your fantasy.
In real life they commit suicide,
find any way to expunge themselves.
They try to keep from taking the blame
for the demises of boys
who claimed their love was infinite.
What do their demises say about infinity?

Don't go asking for an introduction,
I will only be introducing an allusion
to certain illusions which
no one understands anymore.
Every storybook is muddled in muck.
We slip into it, and are sullied.

Of the 3 Alices I've known of,
I am only close to my grandmother.
She is closer only because
she isn't a story character.
Everyone suspects that she asphyxiated
stuffing her lungs with smoke.

Only I know she was trying
to stifle screams that weren't heard.
It's as hard to accept yourself
as it is to carry the weight of a legacy.

LIKE A METEOR
(May 2014)

I know you've been thinkin' about falling
To earth like a meteor.
And I know that you would fall so well, dear.
That yours is the kind of skin that would light up the sky—
Wedding dress white.

But, is it just because you know that you are a catastrophe?
Because we know it too, but we still wait each year
To see you streaking the sky each year.
And you're more than a mark on my calendar.

Stop hoping you can be the crater you leave behind.
You are a moonlit meal for our eyes.
You are more than the red dwarf of your heart.

Some days I want to explode too, sometimes I do.
If you are a comet catastrophe
I can be your gravity.

She looks me up and down and says,
Do not mistake yourself for my bridegroom.
Or me for a widow-maker.
I want to be more than a memory.
You will see me from space written on the land
Like Sanskrit in a Quran.
I am tired of people looking up at me.
This is my annulment from the sky.
There is nothing as hard as being married to the night.
She was reckless, but she was something.

I am tired of the expectation in your telescopes.
I've been waiting to see you in my sky,

Since my father taught me to read the stars.
Astronomers, we love straining our eyes trying to see
The asterisk stars you tie to your tail, like beer cans on a bumper.
I've built pinpoint telescopes trying to see you streak the sky.

Do not marry yourself into a family of meteors.
Mourn the missing space in our telescopes.
You have no right to grieve.
Stars are dead long before you fall for their light.

What you see are pockmarks and scabs, they'll all fade out one day.
I just want to go out fast.
Leave something behind, even if it's dust.
Cause you would fall so well.
She says, you will learn to love my absence.
Even the sky needs breathing spaces.
Even star maps have story-lines, I am just making mine memorable.
Because you sure are that catastrophe you call yourself,
But you're the comet I've marked on my calendar.
She hears this, looks me up and down and says
I want an ending fit for textbooks.
Crash craters so big they make canyons.
And then you can mingle with me, touch my dust
Swim in my ashes in a crater lake.

PART III

POEMS FROM CHILDHOOD

(2000 -2008)

LIONS IN AN ENDLESS WINTER

The rush of another night upon us,
We embrace the chaos,
With all the wanton wickedness of youth.
Fearless and jolt-addicted
We chase away the dawn
Fighting to escape this concrete town
As Time hunts us with bizarre exuberance,
The dark road takes us out, and on, to paradise---
To the world beyond our grey-stoned city.
We are bright young things
Who live in dreams, romancing the night.

Published in "Imagination" 2007

POSTCARD OF DIEGO'S DREAM

Wish you were here,
Overdressed and ostentatious,
In the center of the crowd,
Bone-skinny and beautiful.

      I would watch from the periphery,
An ambiguous face, almost invisible,
In the swarm of honey-colored sycophants.

You'd be perversely enrapturing,
So close to your perfect beauty
That all your flaws come through the cracks
      Between the bones and the empty places
      That used to light up when we smiled.

Writers In The School — Performed 2008

JUST AS LONG AS

Tears dry
Just as long as they have coursed someone else's cheek

Wounds heal
Just as long as they have pierced someone else's skin

Scars fade
Just as long as they have marred someone else's beauty

It won't matter
Just as long as it's not you.

THE GOODBYE

Turn away
Unaffected
Unafflicted
By my tears
Walk into the distance
To the tune
Of some forgotten song
I'll hide my face
You told me not to cry
Tell me I'll forget you
After the goodbye

LULLABY

The music will always last
try not to live in the past
remember there's always tomorrow
and today is moving fast
don't be afraid of anger
don't be afraid of fear
remember I'm always with you
whether we're far or near

Chorus:
and the world may seem so big to you
and the ocean seem so deep and blue
just remember I'm always there for you
and this will always be true

Time doesn't stop at all
live your life big not small
'cause the seasons will keep on changing
from spring to summer to fall
when winter seems so gray
and feels like it won't go away
remember the sun will always shine
each and every day

and the world may seem so big to you
and the ocean seem so deep and blue
just remember I'm always there for you
and this will always be true

and my love will never end
it keeps on flowing like the wind
on and on and on it goes
sharing all the things it knows

you will always grow
learn things you didn't know
and I'll always be right there with you
anywhere you go
I will always love you
and I'll always be thinking of you
whatever you are going through
I'll always be there with you

and the world may seem so big to you
and the ocean seem so deep and blue
just remember I'm always there for you
and this will always be true

Circa 2000
June 13, 2014 Memorial Service
Anita Kruse

FAIRY LAND
(circa 2000)

Do You Remember Fairyland?
Where the sky glittered with fairy dust and fireflies
And the Sugarplums
The Godmothers
The Tinkerbells and Tooth Fairies
All beckoned us to come
Come and join them
Dance and laugh and play with them.
Until the sky laid to rest
And the moon rose to rise

In Fairyland we danced
We twirled and leapt
Two visions in pink
For then we were Fairies
Gorgeous golden Goddesses

But time still passed in Fairyland
The sun still laid to rest
And though little girls
We might have been
Even Fairies don't survive
For as time shall pass
Even little girls must grow too old
To visit Fairyland
So with a grievous sigh
We sighed with grief
 And bid our fantastical Fairyland goodbye